Alfred Waterhouse and the Natural History Museum

Mark Girouard

YALE UNIVERSITY PRESS
New Haven and London
in association with The British Museum (Natural History)

Contents

Published by Yale University Press, New Haven and London in association with the British Museum (Natural History), London

Text copyright © 1981 by Mark Girouard
Illustration copyright © British Museum (Natural History)

Designed by Gillian Greenwood

Filmset and printed in Great Britain by BAS Printers Limited, Over Wallop, Hampshire.

Published in Great Britain, Europe, Africa, and Asia (except Japan) by Yale University Press Limited, London.
Distributed in Australia and New Zealand by Book & Film Services, Artarmon, N.S.W., Australia; and in Japan by Harper & Row, Publishers, Tokyo Office.

ISBN 0-300-02578-5
LC 80-53742

Alfred Waterhouse
and the
Natural History Museum

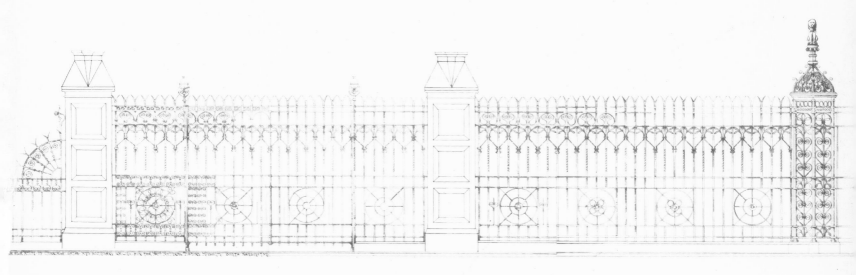

The main sources for the building history of Waterhouse's Natural History Museum are distributed between the Natural History Museum itself, the British Museum, the Public Records Office and the Royal Institute of British Architects. The main committee minutes of the Trustees of the British Museum (the Natural History Museum only acquired its own trustees in 1963) are printed and kept in both Museums. The relevant sub-committee minutes are at the British Museum except for those of 1871 to 1880 (structure, furniture, fittings) which are in the Natural History Museum Library together with supplementary correspondence (structure, furniture, administration) dating from 1873 to 1880. The same Library has Owen's incoming correspondence, his first sketch for a museum, the two volumes of Waterhouse's drawings for the terracotta decoration, and a large collection of cuttings and relevant printed sources. All the relevant correspondence and papers of the Office of Works for the period are in the Public Records Office. All the drawings from Waterhouse's own office are now in the RIBA Drawings Collection and include a great number for the Museum.

The building history of the Museum was first worked out in *The Survey of London, Vol. XXXVIII: The Museums Area of South Kensington and Westminster* (ed. F. H. W. Sheppard, 1975). This has been an invaluable help in compiling this record. Waterhouse's biography remains to be written, and the lack of it is a major gap in the history of Victorian architecture. There is a chapter on him by Stuart Allen Smith in *Seven Victorian Architects* (ed. Jane Fawcett, 1976) pp. 102–21.

Professor Sir Richard Owen (1804–1892), the creator of the Natural History Museum and its first Director. From an engraving based on a photograph taken when he was aged 85. Huxley said of him 'the truth is he is the superior of most and does not conceal that he knows it'.

On 21 October, 1861, Professor Richard Owen, superintendent of the Natural History Departments of the British Museum, in Bloomsbury, London, took William Ewart Gladstone on a tour of his departments. Remorselessly he showed him every square foot of exhibition space, every corner used for storage. With mounting dismay Gladstone realized that both were entirely inadequate. The stores were crammed to bursting with inaccessible specimens, the galleries were overcrowded and badly lit. He left firmly convinced of two things: the Natural History Departments needed a new museum of their own; and Professor Owen was a brilliantly capable man, with whom he saw eye to eye on a great many subjects.

This, of course, was exactly what Owen wanted him to think. He had been agitating for a new museum for three years; Gladstone became one of his most powerful backers and it was during Gladstone's first term as Prime Minister that, in 1873, the new museum finally began to rise out of a hole beside the Cromwell Road – after fifteen chequered and controversial years of campaigning and preparation.

Fifteen years is a long time. If Owen was largely responsible for the final success, the controversial elements in his character may have caused some of the delays. He had a flair for publicity of which his effortless nobbling of Gladstone is a typical example. But he also had a gift for making enemies. 'It is astonishing' T. H. Huxley wrote to a friend in 1851 'with what an intense feeling of hatred Owen is regarded by the majority of his contemporaries. The truth is, he is the superior of most, and does not conceal that he knows it, and it must be confessed that he does some very ill-natured tricks now and then'. Huxley's own relations with Owen were later to run into trouble. Huxley accepted Darwin's theory of natural selection, Owen did not. Huxley was an agnostic, Owen a Christian. At Oxford in 1860, when Huxley demolished Bishop Wilberforce in the famous debate on the origins of man, Owen was supposed to have supplied Wilberforce with his arguments.

But even if he had his limitations, there can be no doubt about his brilliance. He was born in Lancaster in 1804. After apprenticeship to a surgeon-apothecary in Lancaster he graduated in medicine at Edinburgh. In 1826 he became assistant curator of the Hunterian Collection at the College of Surgeons in London; in 1837 he became Hunterian Professor. He went to the British Museum as superintendent of the Natural History Departments in 1856. By then he had established his reputation as one of the most gifted

1
Richard Owen and the idea of a museum

Natural history specimens on the staircase landing of Montagu House, which housed the British Museum before it was replaced by Smirke's building in 1823–47. From the painting by George Scharf, 1845.

comparative anatomists and palaeontologists of all time. His appetite and capacity for research were boundless but he also believed in the value of popularization. He was a renowned and regular giver of public lectures; he contributed to Dicken's magazine *Good Words*; he was one of the moving spirits behind the Great Exhibition, and thought up the idea of those life-size models of prehistoric animals that still lurk so unexpectedly around the lake in the Crystal Palace gardens.

'What with marbles, statues, butterflies, manuscripts, books and pictures' wrote Sir Robert Peel of the British Museum in 1824 'I think the museum is a farrago that distracts attention'. The mixture reflected the character of the original collection formed by Sir Hans Sloane and bought for the nation in 1753. The new buildings designed by Robert Smirke and built in 1823–47 gave the Natural History collection more capacious quarters, but even these soon proved inadequate. There was some feeling that Natural History was not getting a fair deal. It was divided into four departments, of geology, zoology, botany and mineralogy, each with its own Keeper, who dealt directly with the Principal Librarian, the chief museum official. There was no one person to speak up for all four departments. Owen's job was a new one, created in 1856 to provide such a person and balance the impending appointment of Panizzi as joint Secretary and Librarian. The dynamic and forceful Panizzi put books first; he would, as Macaulay commented 'at any time give three mammoths for an Aldous'. But Owen's insertion into an existing power structure had its disadvantages. He had no department of his own; the four existing keepers retained almost despotic powers within their own spheres. They were all distinguished men, and the most distinguished of them, J. E. Gray, Keeper of Zoology, was four years older than Owen. This delicate situation was to influence, and at time confuse the whole development of a separate Natural History Museum.

In 1858, two years after Owen's arrival at the British Museum, 120 eminent scientists signed a memorial to Disraeli, complaining of the inadequate conditions in which the Natural History collection was housed. Owen was probably at the back of this although he did not sign it, no doubt because he was a Museum employee. About the inadequacy there was, in fact, general agreement, but controversy soon started up about how to deal with it. Should the British Museum itself be enlarged, or should a new Natural History Museum be hived off from it – and if so where? And what form should a new museum take – how large should it be, and what proportion of space should be given to display, what to research and storage?

Early in 1859 Owen made a report to the Trustees of the British Museum in which he recommended the idea of a new museum, and included sketch plans to show how it might be organized. In 1860 the trustees (by a small majority) accepted his ideas in principle and voted for removal to the estate of the 1851 Exhibition Commissioners in South Kensington. A site to the

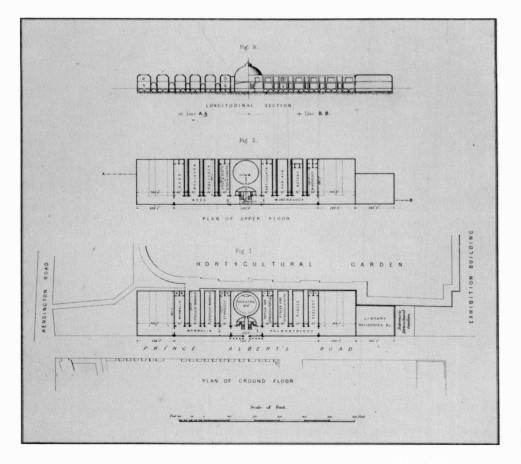

A plan published in 1862, adapting Owen's scheme of a single-storey museum for a more constricted site in South Kensington.

9

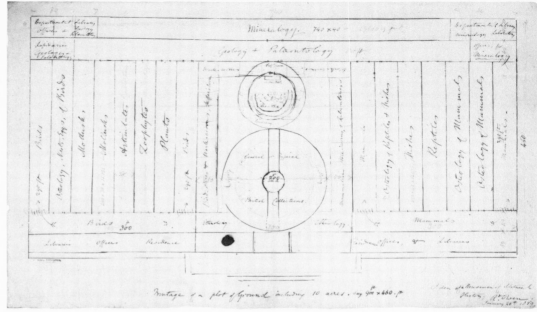

Professor Owen's sketch proposals for his ideal Natural History museum, as drawn by him in 1859, and (below) an alternative proposal published in 1862 for accommodating the Natural History collection by enlarging the British Museum.

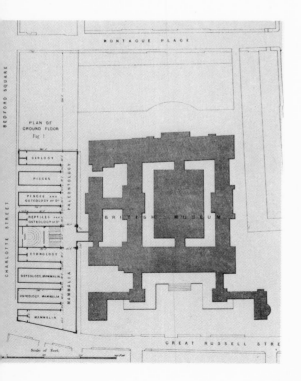

east of what is now Queen's Gate was offered to them, and in 1862 Owen's scheme, revised to fit the site, was published in a pamphlet by him entitled 'On the extent and aims of a National Museum of Natural History'.

The site was never purchased because of the fuss which the project aroused. In the first place South Kensington was still a controversial area. The Commissioners' estate had been bought with the profits of the 1851 exhibition, and ran from Kensington Gore down to Cromwell Road. The moving spirit behind its purchase had been the Prince Consort, who saw it as becoming what in fact it did become: an area dedicated to art and science. The project expressed his confident belief in the value of education, especially as a means of maintaining Britain's leading position in world affairs and of giving working people the necessary tools for self-improvement and responsible citizenship – and thereby preserving the nation from revolution and riot on the recent continental model.

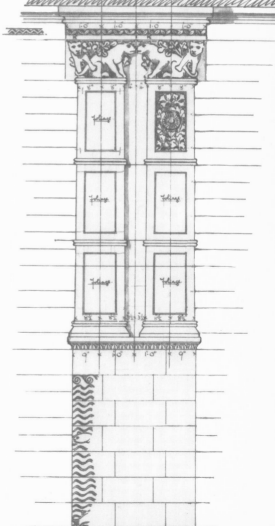

But in 1862 the ultimate success of the project was by no means obvious. What was to become the Victoria and Albert Museum was still an unsightly muddle of miscellaneous buildings; the National Gallery was refusing to be tempted from Trafalgar Square; there were no Science or Geological Museums, no Albert Hall or Memorial, no Royal College of Music or Imperial Institute or College; many of the surrounding terraces were still to be built; the recent death of the Prince Consort had removed the scheme's most powerful patron. The main part of the land between Cromwell Road and the future site of the Albert Hall was occupied by the gardens of the Royal Horticultural Society, and (south of these along the Cromwell Road) by the enormous bulk of the 1862 Exhibition Building, at once less popular and financially much less successful than its predecessor of 1851. To remove a major collection from central London to what was still an outer suburb appeared to many critics a lamentable mistake.

Owen himself had originally been doubtful about South Kensington, but had come round to the idea. 'I love Bloomsbury much' he said 'but I love five acres more'. But his ideas about what to put on the site were as controversial as the site itself. In his original sketch of 1859, and the revised version of 1862, he went all out for a huge museum in which almost everything was on show: 485 100 square feet (44 620 m²) of exhibition space, as opposed to 50 000 (4600 m²) in Bloomsbury. In the 1859 scheme ten acres (4 hectares) are shown covered with top-lit display galleries, grouped round a circular lecture theatre and a circular hall for 'general or typical British collections'. The 1862 scheme had to be shrunk to five acres (2 hectares), but this was done by putting approximately the same accommodation on two floors. There were to be long galleries along the frontage, and short galleries projecting behind them like the teeth of a comb. The space between the teeth allowed light to penetrate to the lower galleries, which were to consist of main, side-lit, galleries under the upper floor areas, with lower and much narrower top-lit galleries between them. The circular hall was now to be above the lecture theatre, and its function was enlarged on. It was to contain two collections. One would 'constitute an epitome of natural history' and would illustrate 'the characters of the Provinces, Classes and Orders and Genera of the Animal Kingdom'; this later became known as the Index Museum. The other would illustrate 'the Natural History of the British Isles'. Both collections were designed to be popular ones, and this part of the museum was to be open in the evening, so that working men and women could come to it.

In 1860 a Parliamentary Committee was highly critical of Owen's ideas. 'An exhibition on so large a scale' it reported 'tends alike to the needless bewilderment and fatigue of the public, and the impediment of the studies of the scientific visitor'. Most scientists, including the heads of the four British Museum departments, preferred the idea of a much smaller area devoted to public display, combined with generous areas for storage and research.

Owen stuck to his guns. He explained his point of view in his 1862 pamphlet. Museums had been designed to amuse or amaze; to teach the uninformed; or 'to afford objects of study and comparison' to specialists. In principle he accepted the last two aims, but went on to specify two more. 'The one Metropolitan Museum of Natural History of a great nation' should display a 'comprehensive, philosophic, and connected view' of all the different classes. Moreover, there was a group between the uninformed and the specialists which needed to be catered for. This included 'the local collector of birds, bird-eggs, shells, insects, fossils, etc. – the intelligent wageman, tradesman or professional man, whose tastes may lead him to devote his modicum of leisure to the pursuit of a particular branch of Natural History'. An elementary display was not enough for people of this type, but on the other hand they were likely to lack the self-confidence or know-how to penetrate to the reserve collections. The more there was on display, the better they would be served.

In effect Owen was appealing to two powerful supporters: national pride and the middle classes. The practical purpose of his intended large-scale microcosm of creation might be debatable; but so huge a display would be a 'material symbol of advance in the march of civilization' befitting the status of 'the greatest commercial and colonizing empire of the world'. And Owen also realized that this commercial and colonizing empire was producing a growing audience of amateur middle-class naturalists, with the time, knowledge and resources to fill glass cases by the gross with birds' eggs, butterflies, minerals or stuffed animals – and to come to his museum to monitor their enthusiasms.

But Parliament was by no means convinced. William Gregory, MP for Galway (whose wife, Lady Gregory, was later to be a star of the Celtic Revival) made a speech regretting that 'a man whose name stood so high should connect himself with so foolish, crazy and extravagant a scheme'. In 1862, although Gladstone and the government supported a bill to set up the new museum on the Queen's Gate site, enough back-benchers voted against it to result in its being thrown out.

Undeterred, Gladstone, supported by a somewhat dubious Owen, tried another tack. This was to buy the 1862 Exhibition Building and put into it, not only the new Natural History Musem but a new Patent Museum, a new National Portrait Gallery, and possibly other museums – thus getting a very large new building relatively on the cheap. A bill to buy the site got through Parliament in 1863, but an ensuing bill to buy the actual building from the contractors, who had erected and still owned it, did less well. Its elephantine heaviness was in striking contrast to the delicacy of the Crystal Palace, and it was much disliked by many people. Once again the back-benchers revolted.

Palmerston, the Prime Minister, described them as 'like an army that has taken a town by storm; they have broken loose from all control.' The Bill was thrown out; the contractors pulled down the building.

But at least the Government now had a site, even if there was nothing on it. It occupied the ground on which the Natural History Museum now stands, but extended a little further to the north. In 1864 a competition was set up to fill it, and assessors were appointed. The projected new building was to be built in two stages – the first half was to contain a Natural History Museum and a Patent Museum; the use of the second half was left unsettled. To the surprise of all, and the amusement of a good many, the winner of the competition was Captain Fowke, RE, the architect of the 1862 exhibition building. There seems, however, to have been no collusion. Most people thought the winning design handsome enough; one of Fowke's assistants, John Liddell, later claimed to have designed it. Even so the British Museum trustees announced that they preferred the plan of the runner-up, Robert

Kerr. Nothing had been decided when Fowke unexpectedly died, in December, 1865.

What were the government to do now? Should Fowke's design be carried out by someone else; or should the commission go to the runner-up? In February, 1865, William Cowper, First Commissioner of Works (the minister in charge of public buildings) announced his decision. Fowke's design was to go ahead; the executive architect was to be a relatively unknown man, a rising star from Manchester, Alfred Waterhouse.

Alfred Waterhouse (1830–1905), the architect of the Natural History Museum, from the portrait by Sir William Orchardson.
RIBA

Alfred Waterhouse was born in Liverpool in 1830. Both his parents were Quakers; he himself does not seem to have remained one beyond early manhood, but his Quaker background was to help him in his career as an architect, and was the main reason why he adopted it in the first place. Waterhouse himself had wanted to become an artist; but to Quakers painting seemed a dangerous and rather frivolous profession, and accordingly architecture was settled on as an acceptable compromise.

He served his articles with Richard Lane, an able architect with Quaker affiliations practising in Manchester. Lane was predominantly a classicist; but Waterhouse, like many of his contemporaries, became an enthusiastic supporter of the Gothic Revival, and an eager imbiber of the writings of Pugin, Scott and, above all, Ruskin. After a year of travel, in which he reached as far as Constantinople and increased his knowledge of Gothic architecture in Italy and France, he set up on his own in Manchester in 1854.

Commissions from Quaker families such as the Barclays, Peases and Binyons helped his practice along; but his abilities were so outstanding that it did not need much help. The real foundation stone of his career came by way of open competition, in 1859. This was the commission for the new Manchester Assize Courts. The resulting building (which was demolished after being damaged in the last war) was praised for its lavishly Gothic façades and striking skyline, but was especially admired for its planning. It established Waterhouse's reputation as a man who could plan large and complex buildings in a manner at once handsome and convenient – and who knew about law courts.

In 1865 Waterhouse moved down to London, probably on the strength of a commission to build a bank in Lombard Street. But London had an even greater attraction for him, in the shape of the imminent competition for the new Law Courts in the Strand. This was to be one of the great English buildings of the nineteenth century – and who was better qualified to build it than Waterhouse?

His specialist knowledge was, in fact, recognized at the end of 1865, when William Cowper, First Commissioner of the Works, asked him to draw up a specification of the accommodation required in the new building. Cowper (later created Lord Mount Temple) was more than a politician; he was a friend of Ruskin, Rossetti, and other gifted Victorians, and employed William Morris to decorate St. James's Palace and W. E. Nesfield, one of the

2
Waterhouse and the realization of the idea

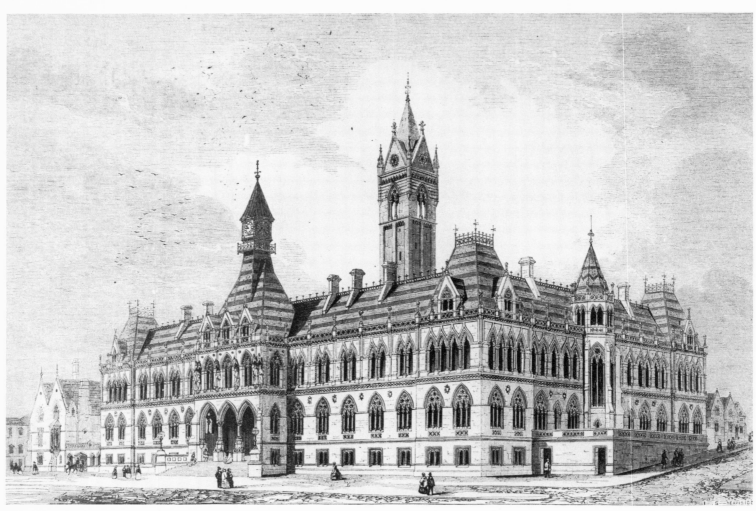

The Manchester Assize Courts, designed by Waterhouse in 1859 in a mixture of English Decorated and Italian Gothic. The Courts (which have been demolished) were the foundation of his reputation as an architect.
THE BUILDER

most interesting of Victorian architects, to design buildings in Regent's Park and on his own estates in Hampshire. He assured Waterhouse that drawing up a specification would not prejudice his chance of taking part in the actual competition. But almost at once he had second thoughts; to obviate any suspicion of unfair advantage, drawing up the specification was to preclude competing. Accordingly, on 31 December, three weeks after he had taken it on, Waterhouse resigned the job.

Details from the main front of the Natural History Museum. The format of the windows was inspired by those in Fowke's museum design of 1864 (p. 14), but Waterhouse changed the detailing from Fowke's Italian Renaissance into Romanesque.

The fact that within a few weeks Cowper asked Waterhouse to carry out Fowke's design for the Natural History Museum suggests that he had been impressed by his tact, efficiency and ability, and perhaps that he felt guilty about the fiasco of the first appointment. At much the same time he and his fellow assessors invited Waterhouse to be one of the architects taking part in the Law Courts competition; this, it had been decided, was to be a limited one. But although the lawyers considered Waterhouse's resulting entry much the best one, he lost the competition to Street; whereas the Natural History Museum, from being a relatively unimportant business of carrying out someone else's designs, developed into one of his most important and best known buildings.

In June 1866 the Liberals went out and the Conservatives came in. The museum project was put into cold storage for eighteen months and when it was revived the Natural History Museum was the only part of it to survive. The Patent Museum had disappeared and so had the space for unspecified future museums which had formed one half of Fowke's design. Waterhouse was still the architect; and, reasonably enough, he was now empowered to

revise Fowke's design if necessary. In effect he designed a new building; but he was careful to leave enough traces of Fowke in it to silence possible criticism.

In March, 1868, Waterhouse submitted his plans. The Trustees of the British Museum approved them, the Government said that they would work out too expensive. Then, in December, the Conservatives went out and the Liberals came back. This should have been good news for Waterhouse, but it only caused further delays. The new First Commissioner, Henry Layard, was an enthusiast for a Natural History Museum – but on the Thames Embankment, not in Kensington. The proposed change of site resulted from a grand project to line the new Embankment with public buildings, including the new Natural History Museum, the new Law Courts and possibly a new national Opera House and National Gallery. It was a magnificent idea, and among much else produced some evocative drawings by Waterhouse for a grandly-domed building following the curve of the river; but for a number of reasons it failed to materialize.

Accordingly, by May, 1870 Waterhouse found himself back with the old site and a new First Commissioner. The latter was to prove as much of a stumbling block as Layard, but for different reasons. He was A. S. Ayrton, whom Sir John Betjeman once described, with some justice, as 'that stinker Ayrton'. Ayrton's main passion was for economy; he despised art, disliked most architects and artists, and felt that one of his main functions was to cut them down to size. Gladstone was believed to have appointed him mainly in order to silence, and possibly in the end discredit, a politician who when out of office had been inconveniently critical. In his years as First Commissioner he badgered poor Street at the Law Courts so unmercifully that he helped to bring about his early death; he nearly shipwrecked Alfred Stevens's great monument to the Duke of Wellington in St. Paul's; and he made life very difficult for Waterhouse. But Waterhouse was not the man to be got down by a First Commissioner, however awkward.

Waterhouse's budget on the Embankment had been £500 000; Ayrton said this must be cut to £330 000. Waterhouse's solution was simple; he redesigned his building to be built in two stages; the first stage came within the cost limit, and was viable as a museum on its own, but lacked the side and rear ranges necessary to make up a proper architectural whole. As such, early in 1871, the design was finally approved; as such, with minor modification it was built, and as such it remains. No doubt Waterhouse hoped that funds would ultimately be found to complete his building, but they never were. Architecturally it has been left to this day with a very grand front, but no back or sides.

If Waterhouse, Owen, or anyone else hoped that their troubles were over, once Parliament and the Trustees had approved the design and Parliament had voted the money, they were in for disillusionment. Tenders were not invited until July 1872, nearly two years after Ayrton had fixed his limit of £330 000. In the interval building costs had rapidly inflated, but Ayrton refused to allow any increase. Waterhouse had to truncate his two entrance towers, reduce the two north towers to one, replace wooden ceilings by plaster ones, drastically reduce the decoration, and make various other economies; even then the lowest tender came out at £352 000, which Ayrton grudgingly allowed.

Work began in the spring of 1873, and did not go smoothly. There were troubles over the delivery and sorting of the terracotta; there were delays in the supply of iron; the contractors, Baker and Son, complained that the architect kept changing his mind. In the summer of 1879, to the accompaniment of mutual recrimination, Baker and Son went bankrupt; they blamed Waterhouse's procrastination, rising costs and delays in the delivery of terracotta. However, their creditors allowed them to finish the contract. Meanwhile the Tories replaced the Liberals and some of the items cut out by Ayrton crept back again. In particular, Captain Shaw, the London Fire Officer, came to the rescue of the entrance towers. These had to contain water tanks which, in those days, provided the pressure for hoses in case of fire. Captain Shaw announced that the towers, as truncated for Ayrton, could not produce the necessary pressure. On this utilitarian argument the full height of Waterhouse's cathedral centrepiece was re-instated.

'As my strength fails' wrote Owen in September, 1879 'and I feel the term of my labours drawing nigh, how I long to see the conclusion of their main aim'. He had eighteen months to wait and there was at least one more drama to come. On 10 March, 1880, a Mr Newton, encouraged by Panizzi, wrote to complain about the statues recently set up at the foot of the great staircase. They were 'paltry and meretricious figures', 'only fit for a second class theatre', 'faulty both in design and execution' and would serve 'to corrupt and degrade public taste'. What on earth were they? Newton's language suggests that they were nude. At any rate the Trustees went in a body to see them, and they were removed.

At last, in April 1881 and only two years before Owen's retirement, the Museum was finally opened to the public.

NATURAL·HISTORY·MUSEUM·

½" scale details of the east side of E. pavilion + W side of W pavilion.

There was no question of Waterhouse's final design being a new creation. It had behind it twelve years' gestation, and bore the marks of Owen's 1859 and 1862 suggestions, of Fowke's competition design of 1864 and of Waterhouse's own first thoughts of 1868. And like all complex buildings it had to reconcile – or attempt to reconcile – numerous different, and often conflicting, requirements and points of view.

When Owen sat at his desk in 1859, and sketched out his ideas for a museum, the scribbled diagram that resulted was conditioned both by ideas special to him and by assumptions common to his age. The enormous area devoted to exhibition space, and its division into a popular section and a much larger area of specialist galleries, reflected his own individual and controversial views about the form a museum should take. The provision of a large lecture theatre was by no means common in museums of the time and resulted from his belief in the teaching functions of a museum and perhaps also from his own popularity and prestige as a lecturer. But the reliance on top-lighting, the rigidly symmetrical layout, the grand central hall and the suggestion of a portico in the centre of the entrance façade were all in tune with the accepted contemporary image of a museum or picture gallery.

Top-lighting was a purely practical matter. Although the South Kensington Museum had pioneered evening opening by gaslight, gas was a substitute for daylight not a supplement to it. In daylight hours museums were still entirely lit by natural light; and it was generally and rightly agreed that for exhibition purposes some form of top-lighting was the best way by which to introduce it. In going in for symmetry and an element of grandeur, on the other hand, Owen was accepting contemporary views about what museums should look like. They had to symbolize the importance of their function, and the status of the nation, city, or potentate who commissioned them. They had, therefore, to look important, and convention suggested that they should do so in a particular way. They were expected to have a symmetrical façade; a central entrance through some kind of imposing frontispiece; and inside a central hall, and, if necessary, a grand staircase to match the pretensions of the exterior. The pedigree of this kind of building went back to the Baroque or Palladian palaces and great houses built in the seventeenth and eighteenth centuries; and the commonest form of central

3
The building

entrance was through a classical portico, with the rest of the architecture to match.

The grand staircase arrived, and the portico was made explicit, in Owen's second scheme of 1862. The staircase became necessary because the first scheme had to be adapted for a smaller site, and therefore be put on two floors. As a result Owen's original requirement of nothing but top-lit galleries had to be compromised; and the need to get light down to the rear galleries on the ground floor suggested the alternation of wide and narrow galleries.

Many elements of the 1862 scheme survived to the end. The placing of general and British Natural History collections and grand staircase in the centre, the mixture of side- and top-lighting, the combination of two (in the end three) storeys of galleries along the front with back galleries at right angles to them, the alternation of wide and narrow galleries – all came to fruition in Cromwell Road. But the lecture theatre disappeared, rather mysteriously, in 1871; and there were inevitable concessions, developments and alterations in the remainder.

Fowke, in 1864, made two vital contributions to the final result – a façade design, and a change of metaphor. His was the first scheme to be worked out in enough detail to suggest a real building, rather than produce a diagram. His exterior elevations were in the style which he and his collaborators had already made familiar in South Kensington. This was a distinctive Victorian version of the early Italian Renaissance, with an especial fondness for round-arched windows and lavish but delicate ornament. Surviving examples are the courtyard of the Victoria and Albert Museum, what is now known as the Huxley Building in Exhibition Road, and the Albert Hall. Although materials seem not to have been explicitly named, the drawings suggested the same combination as in the other buildings: red brick for the plain surfaces, yellow terracotta for the ornamental detail.

Fowke planned his building so that a grand central entrance led by way of entrance hall to an even grander staircase, with a very large lecture theatre beyond it. The architectural form in which he expressed this was the most striking feature of his design. He abandoned the traditional symbolism of a classical temple, entered by a portico, for the symbolism of a christian church or cathedral, surmounted by a dome. The central mass of his building was clearly inspired by Bramante's famous, though never executed, design for

St. Peter's, Rome, made in 1506. Four subsidiary domes at the corners of a square led up to a great central dome, rising above the staircase hall.

To strike this ecclesiastical note was by no means inept; indeed it was soon taken up all over Europe. Victorian museums tended to be built in a dedicated missionary spirit that was in sympathy with their presentation as secular cathedrals. In particular Owen, like his friend Gladstone but unlike his rival and enemy Huxley, believed that the material world revealed the wisdom and purposes of God, who had created it. A Natural History Museum should display and make evident the divine rationality of creation; it deserved to be approached in a reverent and religious spirit.

When Waterhouse set to work on reworking Fowke's design in 1870–1 he was faced with two main problems. Firstly he had to work out a plan that would be acceptable to Owen, the keepers, the British Museum trustees and the Government. Secondly, he had to produce elevations that would satisfy his own preferences and principles without departing too far from Fowke. For he was constricted by the ambivalent nature of his commission, which was to revise Fowke rather than make an independent design of his own. No doubt 'revision' could be liberally interpreted; but the end result had to have some demonstrable relation to the original.

For his plan Waterhouse adapted a scaled-down version of Fowke's central sequence of entrance hall, circular staircase hall and lecture theatre. Fowke had attached his building to the existing south range of the Royal Horticultural Society's garden; Waterhouse did the same and used the latter for offices, study rooms and libraries. But in the planning of the remainder he kept closer to Owen's 1862 suggestions than Fowke had. He took over Fowke's arrangement (which was adapted from the 1862 scheme) and wrapped two storeys of galleries round the south, east and west faces of the museum. But for the inner galleries which these enclosed he followed the 1862 alternation of wide with narrow galleries. He followed it with a difference, however. Instead of two storeys of wide galleries and one storey of narrow ones he provided the exact opposite, no doubt in order to improve the lighting of the lower side-lit galleries.

For the architectural expression of his plan Waterhouse kept Fowke's cathedral centre, although now there were to be two subsidiary cupolas to the central dome, instead of four. He kept, almost certainly (all but a preliminary sketch of the exterior has disappeared) many elements of

*Francis Fowke's design for a Natural History
and other museums, on the site of the present
museum, 1864 (see p. 14).*
V & A MUSEUM

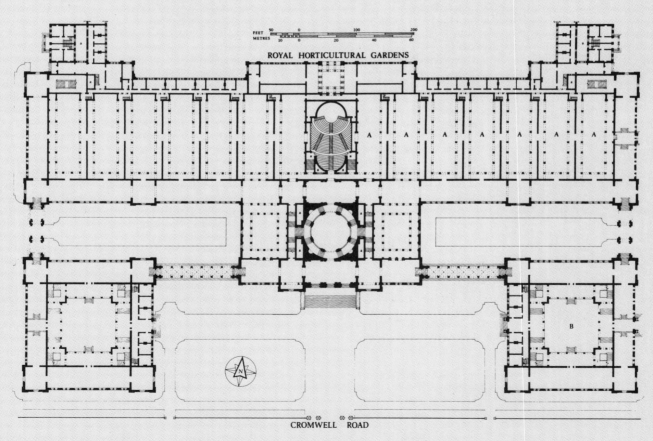

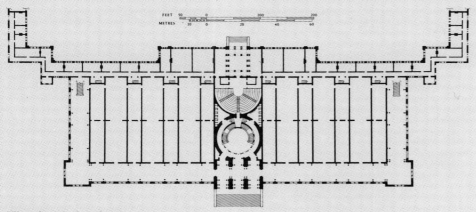

FEET 50 0 100 200
METRES 10 0 20 40 60

Waterhouse's first design, 1870–1.
GLC SURVEY OF LONDON

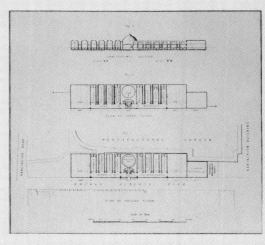

Sketch designs for a site in Queen's Gate, South Kensington, as inspired and approved by Richard Owen in 1862 (see also p. 9).

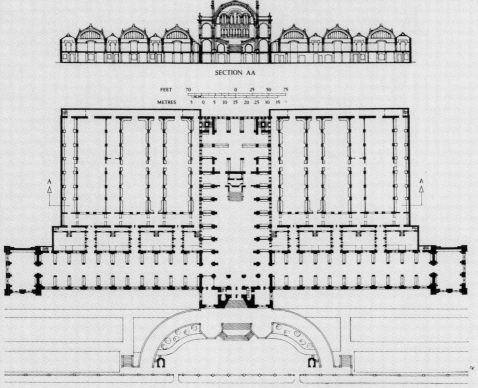

SECTION AA

FEET 70 0 25 50 75
METRES 5 0 5 10 15 20 25 30 35

A

A

CROMWELL ROAD

The plan of the museum as designed in 1871.

*A preliminary sketch by Waterhouse
for his first (1870–1) and unexecuted
design for the Natural History
Museum.*
RIBA

*The section of the 1870–1 design (see p. 29).
Fowke's 1864 design was translated
into a curious mixture of round-arched
Romanesque and painted Gothic forms,
since Waterhouse, like his hero John
Ruskin, heartily disliked the Renaissance.*
RIBA

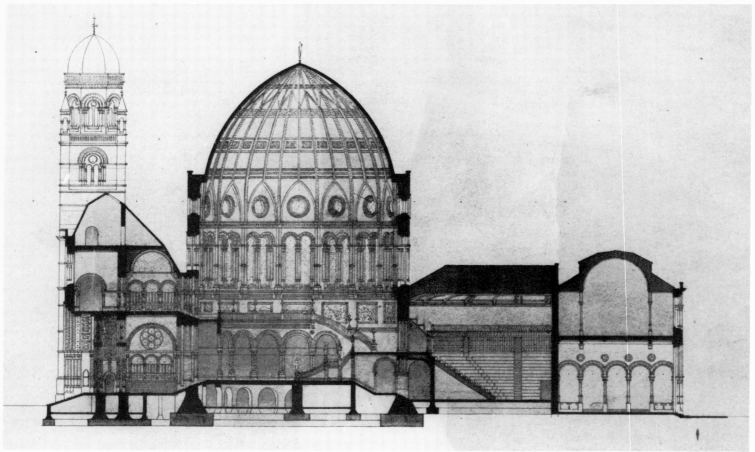

Fowke's façades. But he made one momentous change; he translated Fowke's Italian Renaissance into German Romanesque.

To understand why he did this one has to understand his background. He was still a committed supporter of the Gothic Revival and all Gothic Revivalists were united in the belief that the Renaissance was a disaster. Its roots, they contended, were pagan, not christian. It had replaced the vitality, freedom and colour of the Middle Ages with the tyranny of the five orders. Early Renaissance was slightly better than what followed it, because it still had something of the life of Gothic in it; but it was by no means desirable.

Faced with Fowke's design, Waterhouse was in a situation not unlike that in which Gilbert Scott had been involved with the new Foreign Office in the 1850s, but in reverse. Scott won the Foreign Office competition in 1858 with a Gothic design. Then the Government changed and Lord Palmerston, the new Prime Minister, ordered him to make his Gothic building classical. Poor Scott protested, tried out a Byzantine design as a kind of half-way house, was told that it was a 'regular mongrel affair', finally complied – and was attacked by many of his fellow Revivalists as a traitor.

Scott had been forced to abandon his Gothic design for a classical one; Waterhouse was presented with a classical design which he must have wanted to turn Gothic. But perhaps he felt that the change was greater than some, at least, of the interested parties would stomach; at any rate he went for a compromise. Unlike Scott, however, he succeeded in getting his compromise accepted.

The advantage of Romanesque was that it was palatable to Waterhouse because it was the style from which Gothic had developed; but at the same time it was that much nearer to the classical architecture of Rome (hence its name) and so it was easier to convert Fowke's Renaissance façades into it. His round arches, columns and capitals could be preserved; there was no need to introduce pointed arches, which to the general public provide the essential difference between Gothic and everything else.

Although the main reason why Waterhouse abandoned Fowke's Renaissance was probably because he disliked it, as is the way of architects he was also able to produce reasonably convincing practical reasons for doing so. In the first place he was planning to face his new building entirely with terracotta. It is (or was then) difficult to make terracotta in large pieces, or to avoid minor variations in colour between the different pieces. As a result Waterhouse argued that the even and regular finish thought suitable for a classical building would be hard to obtain. Secondly, moreover, Owen wished to have the building decorated with figures of plants and animals symbolic of its contents; lavish decoration with birds and beasts of all kinds was a feature of Romanesque, but not of Renaissance architecture.

So much for Romanesque – but why German Romanesque? Although Waterhouse spoke out against the tyranny of fashion in architecture, in this particular case he was probably influenced by it. In early Victorian days the Gothic Revival was almost entirely inspired by English Gothic; 'Decorated'

or 'Early Middle Pointed' was laid down by the pundits as the correct style to work in. But during the 1850s architects began to chafe at being confined to English examples; continental Gothic was full of excitements (and a continental sketching holiday extremely enjoyable); Ruskin made even Italian Gothic respectable. So architects, Waterhouse among them, went on their travels and Gothic with a foreign accent became fashionable.

There was one element of Waterhouse's compromise between Gothic and Classical that he probably accepted with pleasure rather than for reasons of policy. The rigid symmetry of his plan derived from Owen by way of Fowke, and showed the influence of neo-classical public buildings such as Owen had known and admired as a young man. Most Gothic Revivalists detested symmetrical plans; they thought them artificial, and tended to make their buildings 'naturally' irregular even when irregularity had no practical advantages. But Waterhouse liked symmetry in both plans and façades; he had already shown this in his Manchester Assize Courts, and was to show it again later in grand formal façades such as those he designed for St. Paul's School in Hammersmith and the Prudential Insurance buildings in Holborn.

II THE FINAL STAGE

Waterhouse's 1868 design was never carried out, and most of the drawings for it have disappeared. His 1871 design was actually built, with only minor modifications, and is still substantially there to give one a vivid idea of his highly individual qualities as an architect.

By 1873, when the museum was at last started, and still more by 1881, when it was finally opened, he had come a long way from the relatively unknown young man who had been introduced to the project in 1866. He was one of the best known and successful architects in England, the designer of Manchester Town Hall and University, of the Prudential Insurance Headquarters and St. Paul's School in London, of the new buildings that dominated Balliol College in Oxford and Gonville and Caius College in Cambridge, of a string of large country houses including the Duke of Westminster's Eaton Hall in Cheshire, and of churches, colleges, clubs, office blocks and public buildings by the dozen. He had made enough money

Manchester Town Hall, designed by Waterhouse in 1868–77. It exemplifies the same taste for symmetry, combined with a lively skyline, which Waterhouse also showed in the Museum.
CITY OF MANCHESTER

to set up as a country gentleman, and to buy an estate and build a house at Yattendon in Berkshire.

It is not always easy to reconcile Waterhouse the practical man, the efficient head of a large office, the mass-producer of enormous and not always lovable buildings, the amasser of an impressive fortune, the man who could manipulate committees and governments, with the Waterhouse who had wanted to be an artist rather than an architect, and whose water-colours and drawings retained a miraculously delicate touch until the end of his career. But both Waterhouses existed, and both are present in the Natural History Museum.

The practical aspect of Waterhouse was what most impressed his contemporaries. He and his fellow Gothicists had, as he himself put it, 'hoped that the Gothic revival would be more than a mere revival – that it would turn from a revival into a growth'. Although almost everyone involved in the Revival accepted this doctrine in theory, Waterhouse took it more seriously than most. For him, making Gothic grow had two major implications. It meant not only accepting but welcoming new types of plan,

34

new materials and new methods of construction. It did not mean actually copying medieval buildings or their details. As he put it in 1859 (when writing about his Manchester Assize Courts): 'wherever I thought that the particular objects in view could not be best obtained by a strict obedience to precedent, I took the liberty of departing from it'. That new buildings should endeavour to depart from past styles altogether was something he was no more prepared to contemplate than the vast majority of his contemporaries.

But whatever their stylistic affiliations, his buildings always look unmistakeably Victorian. His Gothic or Romanesque could never be mistaken for medieval Gothic or Romanesque – nor would he have wanted it to be. It was securely anchored to the nineteenth century by his open use of new techniques, especially of iron or steel construction and terracotta facing. And even if his detail kept more or less to one period, in choosing his motifs and organizing his façades he felt at liberty to wander from century to century.

The romantic artist in Waterhouse came out in three especially noticeable ways: in his skylines, his colouring, and his staircases. He had spent his early professional life in Manchester, at a time when it was probably the filthiest city in the world; before his eyes floated the vision of easily washable façades glowing with colour, and dramatic skylines designed 'to make our buildings effective, even under a gloomy sky'. Once inside, no Victorian architect was more capable of making the move from floor to floor and space to space a dramatic experience.

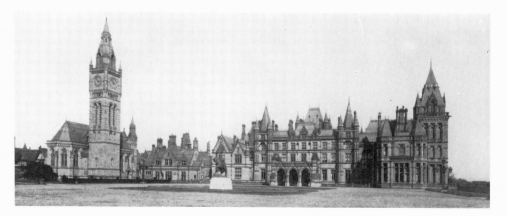

Waterhouse designed a number of country houses of which the Gothic Eaton Hall, in Cheshire, remodelled for the Duke of Westminster in 1870–82, was much the most ambitious.
NATIONAL MONUMENTS RECORDS

The romantic, the practical and the eclectic aspects of Waterhouse are all in evidence as one looks across Cromwell Road at the museum. The regular and remorseless march of round-arched windows along the 680 feet (207 metres) of its frontage expresses the regular grid of iron beams and supporting iron columns that lie behind it. The uncomplicated symmetry of the façade makes clear that Waterhouse, unlike most other Gothic revivalists, refused to inject whimsical irregularities into his buildings when there was no need for them. But he also believed that it was the task of the architect 'to clothe over practical necessities with such beauty as they were capable of receiving'. So over his iron framework he stretched a covering of terracotta, ornamented with birds and beasts, living and extinct, and coloured in a ravishing combination of fawn and pale blue-grey. Above his symmetrical façades he carried his buildings up to the skyline of towers, spires and pinnacles. And he made arriving, entering and exploring the museum as exciting as possible.

He did this by means of Fowke's cathedral motif and Fowke's great staircase hall, translated into German Romanesque, and made far more dramatic than anything Fowke could have conceived. Visitors pass through splendid wrought-iron gates up a broad flight of steps (or, if on wheels, a spaciously curving ramp) to a huge cathedral portal, framed by towers, decorated with carved beasts and twisted columns, and recessed like a cave into the cliff of the front. Through this they come into a hall in scale with the entrance, echoing with the shrieks of excited children. The circular rotunda of earlier designs has become a rectangular cathedral nave, with a triforium above and arcades below, opening into a series of side chapels designed to enshrine Owen's Index Collection; but overhead the unsentimental practical Waterhouse emerges, and replaces the massive Romanesque vault one might have expected with a roof of iron and glass.

What turns the great hall from an impressive space into an extraordinary one is the staircase which has been inserted into the cathedral nave. This starts handsomely but conventionally enough at the end of the hall, in the form of a single broad flight that breaks into two at the landing and climbs up to the triforium galleries on the first floor. The exciting bit is the next stage up to the second floor galleries. To get to these one walks along one or other of the galleries to a bridge that spans the hall by means of a single arch towards the end nearest the entrance. Flights of steps climb up either side of

Waterhouse's drawing for the main entrance to the museum, and (right) the entrance as it was built. 'A huge cathedral portal, recessed like a cave into the cliff of the front.'
RIBA

Three views in the main hall. Its brilliantly unlikely combination of cathedral-style Romanesque arcades, grand staircases in the Baroque manner, and roof and cast-iron columns reminiscent of Victorian railway architecture make it one of the most exciting interiors devised in the nineteenth century. The panels of the roof were painted by Best and Lea of Manchester in such a way that six panels together make up one branch of a tree, climber or shrub.

this. From the top of the bridge a final flight leaps across the gap between the bridge and the end of the hall. The effect is sensational from every point of view. From the top of the bridge, or the head of the final flight, there are bird's eye views down into the hall; from under the bridge there are vistas through into the hall, up between the gaps between bridge and walls to the roof, and to either side along the lofty pillared tunnels of the front galleries. The combination of complex and dramatic spaces with constantly moving crowds is extraordinarily exhilarating.

*A water-colour made by Waterhouse in 1876,
showing the final design for the Museum. The side
façades were never built. The smoking tower at the
rear contains the flue of the central heating system.*
V & A MUSEUM

The Romanesque cathedral at Worms in Germany. A number of German Romanesque churches have towers at both west and east ends, a feature copied by Waterhouse when designing the great hall at the Museum.
DEUTSCHER KUNSTVERLAG

The Liebfrauen Kirche, Andermach, Germany. Waterhouse had seen it, and it probably influenced the design of the central feature of the Museum.
DEUTSCHER KUNSTVERLAG

Its Romanesque styling gives the museum a certain ornamental unity. But since there were virtually no elaborate Romanesque buildings except religious ones, still less any Romanesque museums, Waterhouse was left with plenty of room for improvization. Some of his motifs came, it is true, straight from Romanesque churches. The towers, spires and gable of the entrance suggest the Liebfrauen Kirche at Andermach, which he visited in 1861. The great portal is reminiscent of the Gnadenpforte at Bamberg, which he saw in 1866, and of the north door of St. Jacob's Regensburg. The 'chapel' spaces off the hall probably derive from the similar arrangements at St. Gerion, Cologne. As in a number of German cathedrals (at Worms, for instance) the hall has pairs of towers at both ends, instead of just at the entrance.

But no Romanesque building had a staircase like that at the Natural History Museum; its inspiration is, if anything, Baroque with, perhaps a touch of the extraordinary flying choir screen of *c.* 1545 at St. Etienne du Mont in Paris (Waterhouse had planned somewhat similar bridges to carry the first floor circulation across the great hall in his design for the Law Courts). The round-arched openings without capitals which are such a

distinctive feature of the museum (and especially effective when repeated over and over again in enfilade, as in the corridors connecting the front to the back galleries) are not Romanesque; they derive from late-Gothic churches, with pointed arches turned into round ones. There were no Romanesque precedents for dormer windows; the dormer windows along the entrance front, and the wedge-shaped spires of the pavilion at either end are inspired by French Gothic examples. There was no tracery in Romanesque churches; the simple tracery of circles and semicircles repeated in all the windows of the

A design by Waterhouse for the central feature, very nearly as it was built. The figure of Adam on the central gable was erected, but toppled from its position during the 1939–45 war.
RIBA

first floor galleries is in fact obtained by tricking out Fowke's early Renaissance window designs with Romanesque mouldings. In fact when one compares Fowke with Waterhouse one finds that the basic unit of the façade comes from Fowke: not just the traceried windows on the first floor, but the two round arches set in rectangular frames on the floor below them. And the two end pavilions are recognizably the off-spring of the eight somewhat smaller pavilions which Fowke placed at the corners of his two wings.

A detail design for the first floor windows, made in 1874.
RIBA

Windows on the east pavilion.

45

The four towers and cathedral centre of the museum were carefully placed to look down the central walk of the Royal Horticultural Society's garden to the Albert Hall, also centrally placed at the other end of the garden. When the garden was built over later in the century all the new buildings that replaced it were sited along this central axis, although in fact by blocking the view they made the axis meaningless. One has to go up in an aeroplane (or climb the tower of the Imperial Institute) to appreciate that the four towers of the Natural History Museum, the tower of the Imperial Institute, the two towers of the Royal College of Music, the dome of the Albert Hall and the spire of the Albert Memorial are all neatly lined up with each other.

OPPOSITE *Aerial view of the Natural History Museum, showing its alignment with other major buildings in the area.*
AEROFILMS LTD

III THE PLAN

The plan of the museum as finally built, although recognizably derived from the plans drawn up in 1868, differed from them in a good many ways. Some of the differences had appeared in the design approved in 1871; others came in the course of building.

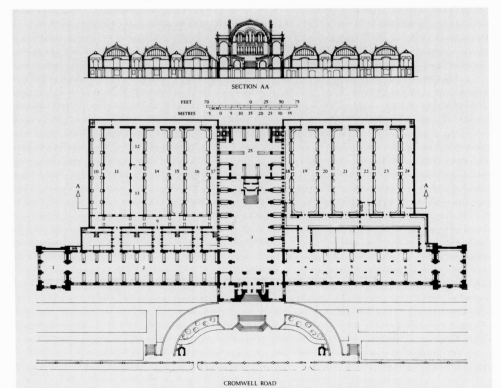

SECTION AA

Plan and section of the Museum as it was finally built. In the right-hand half minor alterations were made to Waterhouse's plan of 1871 (cf p. 29)
GLC SURVEY OF LONDON

CROMWELL ROAD

In the first place, although the site had remained the same the position of the building on it had changed. It had been detached from the Royal Horticultural Society buildings and placed further south, much closer to the Cromwell Road. The ground here was five feet (1.5 metres) below street level; in order that the building should not appear to be in a hole, the main floor was raised above a higher basement than had been originally envisaged; in effect the basement became a lower ground floor, fifteen feet high (4.5 metres).

Secondly, although the concept of a cathedral centrepiece was kept, its form was radically changed. The circular domed staircase hall of 1868 gave way to a much larger rectangular one, designed to contain Owen's Index Collection and the main staircase. A smaller rectangular hall beyond it took the position of the 1868 lecture theatre, and was to contain Owen's British Natural History Collection. The lecture hall had entirely disappeared, as previously mentioned.

Index and British Collections were ideas dear to Owen's heart; the 1868 design seems, somewhat surprisingly, to have made no provision for them and their re-appearance was only to be expected. But the reason for the disappearance of the lecture theatre, which had been another of Owen's favourites, remains somewhat obscure. In 1873 Robert Lowe, then Chancellor of the Exchequer, asked why it had been omitted. He was told that in the view of Owen and Günther (about to succeed Gray as Keeper of Zoology) the Index Museum would be 'sufficient for the purposes of a lecture theatre, and . . . would have the additional advantage that it would contain objects for illustration of the Lecturer's addresses'. The answer did not satisfy Lowe, and it seems unlikely that either Owen or Günther really believed it. Acoustics, arrangement and position made the Index Museum hopelessly inadequate for lectures.

Perhaps the real reason can be deduced from a report made by Owen a week later. He advised the Museum trustees, before they considered how a lecture theatre might be added to the accommodation, to decide 'on the addition to the present duties of certain Officers in the Natural History Department of the delivery of Lectures, as specified in his report of the 10th of February, 1859, and which he again strongly recommended'. It would seem that the heads of departments thought that they had enough to do already without being required to give lectures; perhaps the theatre failed to materialize because Owen's staff did not want to lecture and Owen, now entering his seventies, was no longer able to. In the end nothing was done, and the Museum had to wait eighty years before a theatre was built.

Another major difference between 1868 and 1871 was in the arrangement of the back galleries. Here, some of the changes were made in order to improve lighting levels. More light was brought to the front galleries by dividing the back galleries from them by internal courtyards; and the back galleries were made completely top-lit by omitting the first floor galleries. The loss of exhibition space that resulted was made up by adding an attic floor of front galleries.

Other changes reflected ideas put forward in 1868 by Huxley, repeated in 1870 by P. L. Sclater, the influential Secretary of the Zoological Society, and backed by the Royal Commission on Scientific Instruction. The alternately wide and narrow galleries of the 1868 plan were retained, but the narrow galleries were now to be reserved for students. Reserve galleries were divided from public ones by arches filled with display cases, which the public were to look into from one side and students have access to from the other.

As originally designed by Waterhouse in 1871 the system of rear galleries looked beautifully logical. Display and study galleries alternated; showcases divided one from the other; trap doors led from study galleries to stores in

One of the top-lit galleries in the north-east area at the rear of the Museum, as it is today. It is one of the few galleries which retains its original fittings.
GLC

Another of the rear galleries, as photographed in about 1900.
GLC

the basement; six corridors (three to each wing) led from the front galleries across the internal courts to a communicating cross corridor, and on to the six public galleries; under the six corridors were study-rooms for professors, connected by private staircases to the reserve galleries. In fact by the time the museum opened ten years later almost the whole system had been abandoned.

Owen was unlikely to be enthusiastic about ideas backed by Huxley; and in any case, however good the system looked on the plan, there were practical objections to it. In the eastern half of the museum the Keeper of Geology, G. R. Waterhouse (apparently no relation to the architect) was bitterly critical. In the west J. E. Gray, the Keeper of Zoology, seems to have accepted the system; but he had a stroke in 1869, and gradually handed over more and more to his deputy, Albert Günther, who finally took over from him in 1875. Günther seems to have been as critical as G. R. Waterhouse.

G. R. Waterhouse clearly thought that three connecting corridors were too many, and had no use for the professors' rooms under them; accordingly the latter were scrapped and the three corridors reduced to two, spaced so as to interrupt the front galleries as little as possible. He refused to accept Huxley-type showcases, and the arched opening between narrow and wide galleries were accordingly walled in. In the west, Zoology wing, Waterhouse's three corridors were built as designed in 1871, but the showcase system was abandoned at the end of 1873, when the galleries were half-built.

When the museum opened in 1881 only about one-third of the narrow gallery space was set aside for students; all the rest was for display, and display even extended to the basement where the whales were on show, in not very satisfactory conditions. The arrangement of the main floor of the museum had virtually reverted to what Owen had envisaged in 1859. In this century, when the growing needs of research and storage began to eat up gallery space, wide and narrow galleries were occupied indiscriminately; nothing resembling Waterhouse's system has ever come into operation.

The museum opened with a number of inadequacies. Not only was there no lecture theatre, there was no proper library. The room originally intended as a restaurant (at the back of the British Natural History hall) became a boardroom for the trustees; the surviving refreshment room, although agreeably situated on the first floor between Index and British Natural History halls was (and is) much too small for the needs of the museum. Waterhouse could, however, reasonably argue that the building was unfinished, and that facilities could be added or improved later. The need for a library would have been more pressing if there had been something to put in it; Owen had failed to persuade the trustees to allow the Banksian Natural History library to be transferred from the British Museum to South

Kensington. It was no fault of Waterhouse that, when extra facilities did at length come, no consistent programmes were followed in adding them; so that, architecturally at any rate, the result was chaotic.

The museum had other drawbacks, however. For a visitor its planning was, and is, infuriating. The central spine of the Index and British Natural History halls blocks zoology from geology and divides the museum into virtually self-contained sections. There is only one public staircase; and, splendid as it is as a grand processional way, it is far from efficient as a quick route from floor to floor. A visitor at the north end of what, in 1883, was the fish gallery in the Zoology department was only 150 feet (45 metres) from the north end of the fossil fish gallery in Geology; but if (as was quite probable) he wanted to get from one point to the other, he had to walk well over 600 feet (180 metres). A visitor wanting to get from the fossilized remains of the giant sloth in the south-east pavilion to the meteorites immediately above him on the first floor, had to walk 900 feet (270 metres) – along the ground floor south-east gallery to the central hall, through the central hall and up the staircase, back through the central hall gallery to the first floor south-east gallery, and along that to his destination.

To some extent the divisions reflect the Victorian power-structure of the Museum: little empires, zealously guarded and shut off from each other by their rulers, Gray, Waterhouse and Owen. And yet one can't help feeling that the architect was also to blame: in spite of his reputation as a planner, he was prepared to let the plan suffer for the sake of architectural effect.

Owen regarded the top-lit galleries as the best and most efficient part of the Museum. In the account of it which he gave to the British Association in 1881 he used an evolutionary metaphor. The side-lit galleries expressed the 'character of the primitive and now extinct museum'; the Index hall represented a more advanced species and the top-lit galleries the most advanced of all. But architecturally Waterhouse clearly put the top-lit galleries at the bottom of his scale; for him the stars were the Index Hall, the front galleries, and the great staircase connecting them.

The idea of a grand staircase and side-lit galleries dates from the plan of 1862. They had appeared because Owen's original entirely top-lit and one-storey museum had had to be compressed into a more constricted site. Fowke was given a much larger site, but had to fit four museums onto it. Waterhouse was given the same site for one museum. It was far larger than any foreseeable future needs of the museum could require; the museum has still come nowhere near to filling it. Space-wise there was nothing to stop him going back to something much closer to Owen's original suggestion. Why didn't he – at least in 1870 when he was no longer as constricted by Fowke as he had been in 1868? Instead he even went one step further, and built up the main frontage with three storeys of galleries instead of two.

No doubt one of the reasons was that it is always safer to ask a committee to approve revisions to a design which has already been approved in principle than to send up a completely new design. Yet one also suspects that Waterhouse realized that a one storey top-lit museum would have meant no grand staircase, no great columned galleries, no splendid cliff-like frontage along Cromwell Road.

IV DECORATION, STRUCTURE AND SERVICES

The Natural History Museum was the first building in England, and possibly in the world, where the main façades were entirely faced with terracotta. It was also the first of a long series of such buildings designed by Waterhouse; his enthusiasm for terracotta was so great that it is all many people remember about him.

One of the reasons why he used it at the Museum was that it had already become a distinctive feature of the new buildings in South Kensington. Fowke liked it; so did Henry Cole, the first director of the South Kensington Museum and the moving spirit behind most of what went on in the area; so did many of the craftsmen and designers who worked under them. They liked the technique because it could be used to produce, and if necessary mass-produce, cheap durable ornament from moulds that faithfully reproduced the quality of the model from which they were taken; as Cole put it 'you can have the exact work of the artist upon it'.

But this terracotta was used as ornament not as a facing; the distinctive South Kensington mix consisted of red brick walling set with richly ornamented arches, columns, balustrades and cornices of buff-coloured terracotta. Waterhouse's achievement was to realize that because terracotta was not only cheap and lasting but also resistant to acids and easy to wash, it was an ideal material with which to face entire buildings in dirty Victorian

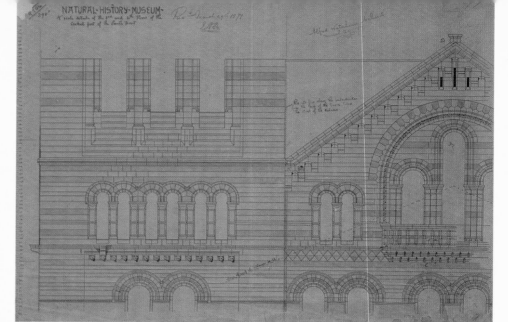

ABOVE, RIGHT *One of Waterhouse's drawings for
the central towers and main entrance.*
RIBA

The main entrance, before and after cleaning.
STONEGUARD

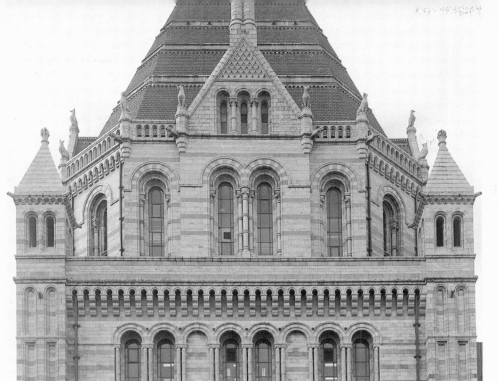

Details of the end pavilions. The corner turrets contain the outlets for the ventilation system.

cities. An experiment in using it in this way had been made in the Huxley building in Exhibition Road, South Kensington (1868–71), where the top floor is faced with terracotta; but Waterhouse went much further. The Natural History Museum required it in such unaccustomed quantities that the sub-contractors, Gibbs and Canning of Tamworth, were unable to deliver to schedule; this, and other problems connected with it, were said to have helped cause the bankruptcy of the main contractors.

Two qualities of terracotta thought by most to be defects were actually attractive to Waterhouse. It was apt to twist if cast in large sections, and pieces tended to vary slightly in colour. Waterhouse liked the irregularity obtained by using smaller pieces, and was especially delighted that 'the fire would at once give us those beautiful accidental tints of which we might avail ourselves if we chose boldly to use them'. In fact he worked in terracotta as a kind of architectural equivalent of painting in water-colour, which was one of his favourite media.

To preserve the freshness of its colouring terracotta needs to be washed at regular intervals, as Waterhouse intended. Dirty terracotta is extraordinarily unattractive; but for many years the Natural History Museum and other

buildings by Waterhouse were left unwashed and their architect was castigated for using so repellent a material. It was not till the museum was cleaned in 1975 that his sensitivity was triumphantly vindicated.

Of course Waterhouse's interest in the facing qualities of the material did not mean that he was not equally aware of its qualities as a form of ornament. From the start he and Owen intended that the building should be rich with terracotta and other decoration, carefully designed to supplement the teaching of the exhibits (at the time some critics said that, rather than supplementing, it confused it). Waterhouse himself made drawings, on the basis of material supplied by Owen; the terracotta was then cast from models made by M. Dujardin, who worked for Farmer and Brindley, the architectural modellers. The ornament was divided into two main classes; the west, zoological, half was decorated with living specimens, the east, geological half with extinct ones. The parapet over the main entrance was originally intended to be surmounted by statues of Adam and Eve, making the point that mankind was the crowning glory of creation. Eve dropped out when the design was changed from a level parapet to a gable; Adam survived on the apex of the gable until he tumbled off (some say deliberately pushed)

in the course of the last war.

In his use of ornament, as in other ways, Waterhouse was not only expressing his preferences and Owen's, he was carrying out the teachings of Ruskin, who had been one of the formative influences on his development. Ruskin believed that different materials should be combined to make glowing patterns of different colours; that 'mere buildings' could only be raised to the status of architecture by being decorated with sculpture; and that one of the functions of sculpture was to teach. He illustrated his ideas with sensitive drawings imbued with a feeling for delicate variations in shade, line and colour. Waterhouse's drawings at his best are equally sensitive; and he never did better than in his designs for the decoration of the Natural History Museum. These are preserved in the Museum library, and fill two volumes of exquisite drawings, into which he seems to have poured much of his frustrated energy as an artist. The resulting statuary, beautifully integrated into its Romanesque setting, provides one of the great pleasures of walking round the museum. Everyone will have their own favourites; perhaps the line of extinct monsters along the eastern parapet, the climbing monkeys in the great hall and the dodo in the east gallery above it are especially memorable.

OPPOSITE *Monkeys in the main hall.*

Waterhouse's drawing for the dodo in the east gallery of the hall.

The south-east gallery on the first floor. These front galleries were fireproofed by a combination of iron columns clad in terracotta, and concrete vaults supported by iron beams, all masked by plasterwork.

The more elaborate figures were only cast once, but many of the simpler motifs were repeated many times. The double rows of square piers along the front galleries are especially nicely detailed. Their lower portion is decorated with tiles of low-relief 'fish' swimming through gently-incised ripples; above four little pilasters give the piers something of a François Ier air. The lower portions were designed to line up with exhibition cases, placed between pier and wall to either side of a central gangway, like bookshelves in a library; the original arrangement still survives in the lower south-west gallery.

The square piers are not purely ornamental; they contain iron columns of H-section which support the ceilings. The terracotta is not there just to conceal the ironwork, but to protect it from fire. Above the piers are what the Victorians called fire-proof ceilings, made up of shallow vaults of concrete supported by iron beams; Waterhouse deliberately displayed the shape of the iron and concrete structure, although he embedded it in a decorative coat of plaster. A further precaution against fire was provided in the form of iron shutters, the slots for which can be seen in some of the

Marine life on the bases of the columns in the front galleries.

61

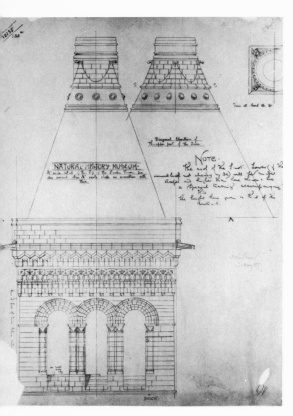

A detail drawing for the central heating 'smoke tower' at the back of the hall.
RIBA, *also opposite*

arched openings. The Index and British collections, and the ground floor front galleries, were designed to be gas lit and open to the public after dark; the shutters were to seal the gas-lit galleries from the rest, which only had daylighting. Finally, up in the octagon lanterns of the two entrance towers are the water tanks insisted on by Captain Shaw.

The square open-work pinnacles around the base of these octagons conceal the openings of ventilation shafts, which run down the piers beneath them; there is a similar arrangement on the south-west and south-east pavilions. The shafts are connected to ventilation openings concealed in the dwarf-arcading around the top of the galleries; the air at the base of the shafts was heated, causing an up-draught which assisted the ventilation. The back-galleries were connected to similar shafts running up staircase wells in the two northern towers. The well in the north-east tower also took the flue from the hot-water heating system, the boiler for which was under the British Natural History hall. This tower is in effect a chimney-stack, with a staircase wrapped round it; smoke can be seen pouring from its flat-topped cap in a perspective drawing of the museum by Waterhouse (p. 40). In this typically Victorian way functional features were made ornamental or at least ornamental features were given some functional justification. The octagons at the top of the south-west and south-east pavilions contained workshops – not, perhaps, in the most practical position.

The top-lit galleries have roofs of iron and glass; but daylighting comes from the lower slopes of the roof rather than directly overhead, an arrangement pioneered in the Hunterian Museum while Owen was working there, and generally regarded as the best one. But many of Waterhouse's careful arrangements for daylighting became gradually redundant once electricity was introduced between 1900 and 1914 (but they may come into their own again). Similarly, most of the original exhibition cases have been dismantled, although a few survive here and there. Some were designed by Waterhouse, others by Sir John Taylor, surveyor to the Office of Works. Much the most elegant survivors are in what used to be the coral gallery, across the internal courts from the ground floor west gallery; these were designed by Waterhouse in 1878. In June 1881 Waterhouse designed a separate building to house objects preserved in spirit, which has been demolished; in 1883 he designed semi-detached houses for a resident engineer and messenger, which still stands between the museum and Queen's Gate.

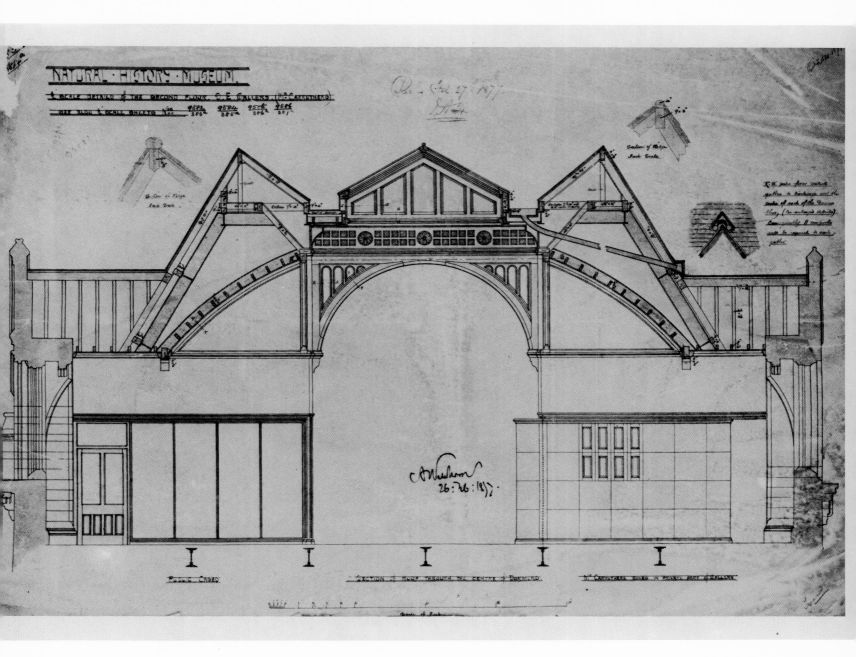

Owing to Ayrton's economies, there was less decorative work than had originally been intended. The painted ceilings, including the lively flower panels in the central hall are by Best and Lea, of Manchester. The mosaic pavements are by Burke and Company; the ironwork, including the splendid entrance gates and railings by Hart, Son, Peard and Company.

In 1887 Waterhouse captured over 90 per cent of the votes in an opinion poll, held by *Building News* to establish the leading British architect. By the time of his death in 1905, his position seemed unassailable. The enormous number of buildings designed by him included in addition to those already mentioned, The National Liberal Club, University College Hospital and the Surveyor's Institution in London, numerous branch offices for the Prudential Insurance, Owen's College (now the main University Building) in Manchester, the Metropole Hotel in Brighton and, among country houses, Blackmoor in Hampshire, Iwerne Minster in Dorset, Hutton Hall in Yorkshire and interiors of Heythrop House in Oxfordshire. He had been given the Gold Medal of the Royal Institute of British Architects in 1878, and was its President from 1888 to 1891. He belonged to many foreign academies and was asked to act as an assessor in architectural competitions.

In 1911–13 six years after his death, designs for east and west extensions to the Museum were prepared, following his style and duplicating his two pavilions. They were never built owing to the First World War. In the 1920s the inevitable reaction began to set in; Waterhouse, along with the whole of Victorian architecture, fell into disrepute. Today his reputation is once more on the rise, and the Natural History Museum has come back into its own.